Immersive Van GOGH Exhibit

This is a LIGHTHOUSE IMMERSIVE INC Publication

Immersive Van Gogh Exhibit

Publishers:	Corey Ross, Svetlana Dvoretsky, Slava Zheleznyakov
Artists:	Vincent Van Gogh, 1853-1890; Massimiliano Siccardi
Writer:	Richard Ouzounian
Book Design:	Vladimir Kevorkov
Photography:	Vladimir Kevorkov, Roman Boldyrev, Patrick Hodgson
Editor -in-chief:	Natasha Abramova
Copy Editor:	Michael Ross
Printed by	The Incredible Printing Group of Companies

Printed in Canada, 2020
ISBN: 978-1-989712-00-9

The publisher would like to thank Bridgeman Images, New York, USA, and akg-images Ltd, London, UK, as well as the museums and archives cooperating with these agencies for providing permissions to reproduce the images in this book. Unless stated otherwise, the copyright for the illustrated works is owned by the collections and institutions listed in the picture captions.

Who Is Vincent?

If you ask ten people at random what they know about Vincent Van Gogh, they would probably tell you ten different things.

"He was an artist."
"Don McLean wrote a song about him."
"He loved sunflowers."
"He lived in a yellow house."
"Kirk Douglas played him in Lust for Life."
"He fought with Paul Gauguin."
"He cut off his ear."
"He went to an asylum."
"He painted The Starry Night."
"He committed suicide."

All of these facts are true, but they only begin to sketch the broadest outlines of the tortured story behind the existence of this man who remains one of the central figures in Western art.

Van Gogh didn't begin painting until he was 27 and died 10 years later, but during that brief

lifetime, he created over 2,000 works of art, including the nearly 900 oil paintings on which his reputation rests.

There have been many biographies of him, which try to make some order of his life, assigning blame to his family and his strict religious upbringing.

And there are numerous catalogues of his art, where you can look at the works in chronological order and try to use them as a key to break the code of his lifelong mental unrest.

But what Massimiliano Siccardi and Luca Longobardi have brought here is completely different.

To begin with, it is not a conventional art exhibition, where the paintings hang on a wall, while you walk

by them and connect the dots in your own mind at the end.

It is a unique combination of art, music and cinemaphotography that Siccardi has been developing for nearly 30 years from humble beginnings with a single slide projector to the technical wizardry you are about to experience.

This is called *Immersive Van Gogh* with good reason. The projected images and haunting musical soundscape will surround you and make it impossible for you to react passively.

Siccardi wants you to understand – no, to feel – what the act of creation must have been like for Van Gogh. Images assemble themselves before our eyes from darkness, with a line here, a splash of colour there, until the painting finally reveals itself.

And all the while, Longobardi provides you with music that stirs your senses further. Sometimes classical, sometimes original, sometimes from the world of modern song, dipping into sources as diverse as Edith Piaf and Thom Yorke.

Are the paintings presented in chronological order? Yes and no. Although the overall arc of the presentation passes through the major places of Van Gogh's career – Antwerp, Paris, Arles,– the paintings do not necessarily appear when they were created. Rather it is as though we see them as they emerge from Van Gogh's consciousness at a particular point in time.

And when is that point? Could it be in the last moments of the artist's life? Or during the day to day struggle that existence became for him in his final years?

Perhaps the answer can be found in Van Gogh's own words: "I dream my painting and I paint my dream."

Massimiliano Siccardi

Artistic Director

Massimiliano Siccardi studied at the London School of Contemporary Dance. But in 1990, he left the world of dance to begin a new journey in the world of video art. Massimiliano quickly became a widely acclaimed artistic force creating video projections for the ballets of numerous choreographers around the world.

He also created video scenography for numerous prestigious international festivals and galas, as well as re-constructed the video mapping of the Basilica di Giotto and the Teatro Petruzzelli of Bari.

Massimiliano is also a celebrated photographer and a professor of digital image elaboration at the Accademia di Comunicazione e Immagine of Rome.

Since 2012, he has been artist in residence at the Carrières de Lumières - Atelier des Lumières where he authored the mise-en-scène of numerous immersive shows inspired by the work of painters like Monet, Chagall, Klimt, Picasso, Bosch, Bruegel and – most notably – Van Gogh.

He is currently creating projects throughout Italy, as well as in New York, Berlin and Leipzig.

Luca Longobardi

Composer

Luca Longobardi (Composer) graduated in Piano, Composition and Electronic Music at the Conservatorio San Pietro a Majella in Naples, then went on to the Manhattan School of Music in New York, where he obtained his Bachelor of Music in Piano Performance cum laude in December 2000.

He obtained a PhD in 2011 at La Sapienza University in Rome in Digital Technologies and Methodologies for Research on Performance in the Department of Art History and Entertainment.

In 2012 he started working with Massimiliano Siccardi, curating the musical choices and writing the original soundtracks for the immersive shows of Carrières de Lumières in Baux-de-Provence, going on to become the musical resource for similar shows around the world.

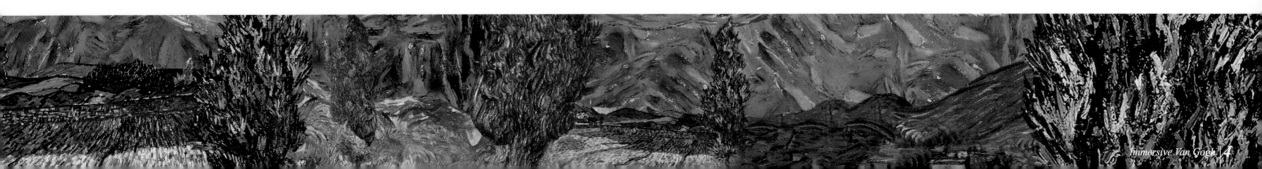

Questions to Massimiliano Siccardi:

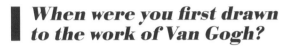

When were you first drawn to the work of Van Gogh?

When I was a child my mother collected prints of the greats of painting, Van Gogh among them, and I was always drawn to his works. I couldn't fully understand the subjects at that young age, but the expressive power of his colours – yellow in particular – and the almost mythical tales of his madness drew me to him.

In 2010, I worked on my first Van Gogh project, which mainly dealt with his time in Arles with Gauguin and then in 2018, I was commissioned to do a new work on Van Gogh, but was instructed to concentrate on the "beautiful" territory, leaving out the "crazy" part that particular producer considered too strong for his audience.

Last year, thanks to Marco Realino who has woven and managed these relationships, I had the first meeting with Corey and Svetlana in Toronto and told them that I wanted to do a new work on "Vincent" and not on "Van Gogh". It was clear to me that the madness I had always instinctively glimpsed in his brush strokes had to come out powerfully with a story that had as its focus not just the man of art, the man of vision, but also the man with his demons.

What made you decide to undertake such a massive examination of his life and works?

I had a clear concept: we see what Vincent sees, we live his experience, we are Vincent in the instant before he dies.

For this reason, the structure of our work is not chronological but starts from that fateful moment, giving us the opportunity to experience his way of looking at the world, knowing all of its desolation and its magnificence.

As he wrote in a letter to his brother Theo, "I see the world in all of its violent beauty... as no one sees it but me."

Why did you feel an immersive presentation was the best way to illuminate Van Gogh to us?

The work of the last 20 years in immersive art has allowed me to experiment in huge and interesting spaces and the opportunity to refine this visual language.

Immersive Art can push the borders of art into more personal experience. The viewers live in the space and with their mere presences modify the perception of the work.

This medium for me is pure emotion. We leave the mind free to welcome the new and the beautiful along with the crazy and the violent.

My past as a dancer, choreographer, director and photographer is all in this work where the imagination is as fluid as a solo of a man alone in the middle of the universe.

What would you like us to feel about Van Gogh after seeing this exhibit?

I wish everyone could see him with a soul free from hidden thoughts. I wish their vision could be both light and dark. I would like everyone to leave the exhibition and say "Hello Vincent. It's nice to have met you on the journey."

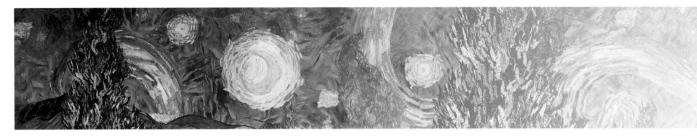

Questions to Luca Longobardi:

When you contemplated providing music for this exhibit, what was your initial thought?

The soundtrack of the work follows two narrative concepts: the emotional condition of the artist and his externalization of that emotion in the creative act. The clear image of a Van Gogh who frequently searches for the complicity of other artists but who then finds exclusive condition in solitude, is the constant that unites the two concepts.

It is only in creation that he can grow beyond solitude, through the repetition of the stroke, in the thickness of the paint on the canvas, in the variety of colors. This artistic multiplication process is represented in music from the choice of pieces for solo instrument or ensemble, for choir or solo voice, for piano or synthesizers, for strings or symphony orchestra. And while the tools come together to create timbres ever richer and more complex, a new meaning insinuates itself to retain the timelessness of his art, but still appear in a totally contemporary production. This moves everyone, regardless of age or culture towards a wider concept of fellowship.

What made you pick songs like "Je ne regrette rien" and "Dawn Chorus" to use in the particular places you did?

I have always instinctively associated the piece by Edith Piaf with the painting *The Sower* of Van Gogh: the introduction of the brasses, the 12/8 rhythm, the text and the inflection of the voice have, in my opinion, a unique location in each brush stroke and color of the work, especially with yellow, which we know to be crucial in Van Gogh's artistic research. The phrase "I do not regret anything" repeated in the song is the same sort of statement that encompasses Van Gogh's search for a life to be lived without question.

Thom Yorke's song is one of the most intimate contemporary ballads I have ever had listened to: the way in which the timbre of the synthesizer is combined with the lyrics in the song moved me from the first listening. I thought of a special place to listen to it surrounded by the silence and I found it in Vincent's *Bedroom in Arles*.

What is the final musical statement you are making at the end of the work?

Immersive art is a very complex concept in that it is not just a technical way to represent the audio-visual experience in huge spaces. The word "immersive" also indicates a deep commitment to intentions that link images and sounds so that the public can experience one different perception of art. Music does not "dominate" images but, on the contrary, allows an approach different, more personal and intimate. The soundtrack of this show is intended as a reminder to the involuntary memory (to use Marcel Proust's concept) that can allow people to generate new specific attachments, to experience a new "madeleine" moment.

Van Gogh's Life

Vincent Willem Van Gogh was born in the town of Groot-Zundert in the Netherlands on March 30, 1853, named after his grandfather and – most tellingly – a brother who was stillborn a year to the day before Vincent's birth.

Van Gogh's father was a minister of the Dutch Reformed Church and his grandfather was a clergyman as well. His mother came from a prosperous merchant family in The Hague and always believed in the importance of keeping up appearances, even on a minister's salary.

The unhappy youth's childhood was turbulent, with his parents frequently sending him away to schools where he was miserable. But he wasn't much happier at home, caught between the rigid religiosity of his stern father and the controlling efforts of his dominating mother.

Much later, he recalled those times in a letter to his brother Theo, who was four years younger, as "austere and cold and sterile," primarily blaming his father, whom he remembered for "a certain steely hardness and icy coldness."

Although drawn to art at an early age, Van Gogh tried to please his family by immersing himself in business, then religion, working as a missionary in the Belgian coal mines, but failing at all he tried.

This period in his life came to an end around his 32nd birthday, when his fiancée attempted suicide after his family forbid their marriage and his father died suddenly of a heart attack.

Van Gogh said goodbye to the stifling atmosphere he had endured all these years and painted his first great canvas, *The Potato Eaters*, as a summation of all that helped to form him, for better or worse.

He moved to Antwerp and spent a frustrating year, starting a damaging pattern of living in near starvation and working without sleep. He enrolled at the Academy of Fine Arts in Antwerp but wound up quarreling with all his teachers, strict traditionalists, who expected him to work on the classical lines that had governed painting for hundreds of years.

He finally broke away to Paris, where he moved in with Theo, who was his financial and emotional support for most of his remaining life.

While establishing himself in the city, he began to acquire a network of fellow artists and friends, which was an anomaly for the solitary Van Gogh. He briefly became obsessed with the craze for Japanese art which was dominating the city and painted several canvases in that style.

He also found himself adopting the brighter colours and more dynamic techniques of the Impressionist and Pointillist artists of the period – Cezanne, Seurat, Signac – and, most importantly, Paul Gauguin, who was to have a tremendous impact on his life.

The years in Paris were an important time of growth for Van Gogh, but his heavy drinking and constant socializing wore on his health and his relationship with his brother Theo deteriorated.

For all those reasons, Van Gogh moved 600 km to the south to the town of Arles, hoping the climate would improve his health and dreaming of establishing a colony of like-minded artists who could live and create together.

Van Gogh only lived in Arles for 15 months, but it was the most creative period in his life, yielding 200 oil paintings and over 100 drawings and watercolours. Initially, he seemed more content

OVERVIEW

than he had ever been in his life and his work bursts with an ever-growing command of colour.

But Van Gogh soon became obsessed about Gauguin joining him there and helping him to establish his colony of artists. He made extensive preparations and leased the famous Yellow House, furnishing it for Gauguin's eventual arrival, which took place on Oct. 23, 1888.

The two men painted together happily for a while, but before very long, their relationship grew strained. Van Gogh had never been fortunate in his dealings with men. He and his father had fought constantly, he rebelled against any employer he ever had and stormed out of the Academy in Antwerp rather than obey his instructors. Even his beloved brother Theo and he quarrelled bitterly many times over the years.

Gauguin and Van Gogh began fighting over everything – women, art, money, the way the Yellow House was being kept. Finally, after a growing period of tension, one night Van Gogh threatened Gauguin with a razor.

On Dec. 23, Gauguin checked into a hotel, fearing for his safety, and that night Van Gogh severed his own left ear with the razor. Gauguin left Arles soon after. Van Gogh spent weeks in and out of the hospital, suffering from delirium. His physician, a young man named Felix Rey, feared for his sanity as well as his health.

Finally, Van Gogh committed himself to the Saint-Paul de Mausole asylum in Saint-Rémy on May 8, 1889, hoping to find peace behind the walls of the former monastery.

Van Gogh seemed to improve during his initial months in the asylum and painted some of his most famous works, including *The Starry Night*.

But his condition soon declined. He began to sink into a state close to catatonia and became obsessed with the thought that he must depart if he were to survive. Against all advice, he left the asylum after a year and moved to the Paris suburb of Auvers-sur-Oise to be treated by Dr. Paul Gachet, who had worked with other artists.

While there, he broke into one last burst of creative activity and completed over 70 oil paintings in slightly more than two months. Van Gogh found himself drawn to the wheat fields outside of Auvers-sur-Oise, writing to his brother Theo that he related to their "sadness and extreme loneliness. The canvases will tell you what I cannot say in words."

Day after day, he would force himself out to the fields, battling scorching heat and swarms of insects, to paint some of his greatest, but most tortured canvases.

Finally, on July 27, 1890, while painting in those fields, Vincent Van Gogh shot himself in the chest with a revolver and died just over a day later from an infection caused by the wound. According to Theo, the final thing he said was "The sadness will last forever."

But Vincent was wrong. Within a decade, international exhibitions had made him a highly esteemed figure in world art and, as more became known about the tragic circumstances of his life, his painfully empathetic work served as an inspiration

for millions of souls.

Massimiliano Siccardi, the Artistic Director of *Immersive Van Gogh*, describes that phenomenon: "Vincent. Let us call him by his first name, since we are his friends and will inhabit the whirlwind of his thoughts.

We will immerse ourselves in his colours. We will be enraptured and enchanted by the substance of his dreams, by the boldness of his strokes, overwhelmed by his passion.

Vincent, that genius in madness, is the representation of a tangible, pulsating contemporaneity that we all share and he casts a light on our disturbed perception of reality.

Contemporaneity is the keystone of our tale's architecture: a representation of a man living through his art every day, suddenly evading the routine, imagining voices and shadows that mirror his most intimate dreams.

We all are Vincent in our daily actions, as we cast a tender look upon this illuminated planet and its stories of violent beauty.

His invitation is for us to look beyond what's clearly visible, longing for an ageless emotional turmoil that strikes us as soon as we raise our eyes towards a never-finished starry night."

We begin in darkness, which is only right, since Massimiliano Siccardi wants us to feel that "we are Vincent in the instant before he dies." There is a low buzzing sound, growing in intensity as the handwritten name "Vincent" appears in blood-red against the background.

The buzzing grows and a giant winged insect startles us. Then images faintly struggle to make themselves seen: a painter's easel... a row of candles... and Vincent, his eyes shining in the darkness, wearing the hat garlanded with candles that he is said to have worn to assist him in painting all night.

Although suffering the effects of a year in an asylum, he painted 70 oil canvases in as many days on an incredible wave of manic energy. He struggled with heat and wind and rain, returning without fail every day to paint in the wheat fields of Auvers-sur-Oise that came to obsess him in those final days of July.

But then there were the insects: flies, cicadas, wasps, surrounding him in blinding clouds that also deafened him because of their tremendous buzzing… He wrote to his brother Theo about one particular trying day when "I picked nearly four hundred flies off the surface of this canvas." No wonder that their presence haunts him in this vision of his final moments. And the words that also pass through his mind in mad disarray?

Vincent wrote 30 letters – almost all to his brother Theo – in the final two months of his life. The last one was unfinished and stained with blood from the gunshot he self-inflicted on July 27.

It stopped after these words: "Well, I risk my life in my job and I almost lost my mind and that's fine."

"Lust for Life" (1956) Kirk Douglas
as Vincent Van Gogh in the Hat With Candles

Three Cicadas | Ink on Paper
1889 | Saint-Rémy-de-Provence, France | Van Gogh Museum Amsterdam, The Netherlands

Self-Portrait with Grey Felt Hat | Oil on canvas. 38 x 44 cm
Winter 1887-1888 | Paris | Van Gogh Museum Amsterdam, The Netherlands

Prologue
Inhabiting the Mind

Space as the scene of creation, as the container of a Joycean stream of consciousness, space as the chosen place where thoughts about light and shadow run after each other, where the image takes shape and disappears, it repeats itself and transforms itself into an almost everlasting black and white.

Space is the instant holding the whole of the human existence.

«Well, I risk my life in my job and I almost lost my mind, and that's fine.»

Vincent Van Gogh in his letter to Theo Van Gogh, Nuenen, July 23, 1890

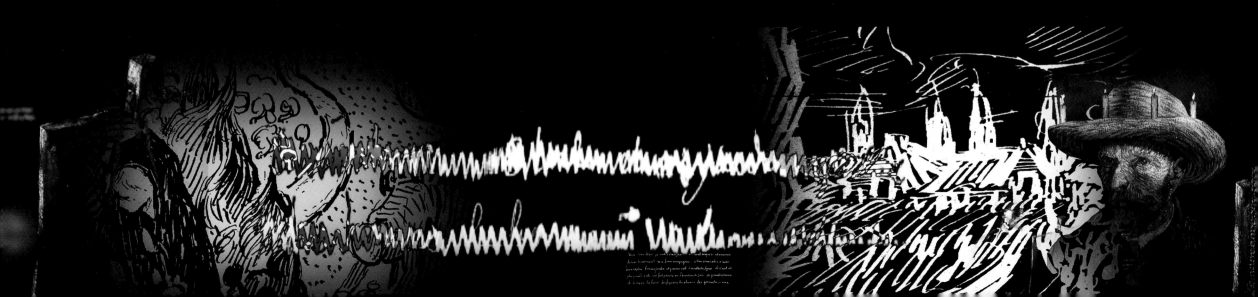

After the ominous beginning of the Prologue, it might seem strange to suddenly explode into Van Gogh's brightest, happiest works – his sunflowers, but there is truly method to this madness.

Before starting on the painful journey through his life, Vincent chooses to remember when he was happiest: his early months in Arles, anticipating the arrival of Paul Gauguin, with whom he hoped to create a colony of artists.

Vincent had actually painted some sunflowers in Paris in 1887, when he and Gauguin first met. The older artist was so impressed with Vincent's sunflowers that he purchased two of them.

Sunflowers became a symbol of Vincent's feelings about Gauguin, and in anticipation of his arrival in Arles in 1888, he painted a famous series of sunflowers proudly upright in a vase. There is hope and anticipation and promise in every painting.

But the time the artists spent together in Arles (in a yellow house chosen by Vincent) quickly turned sour and ended with a bitter fight, Van Gogh cutting off his left ear with a razor and Gauguin returning to Paris. Vincent spent considerable time in a hospital, suffering not just from his injury but from what his doctor felt was a complete mental collapse.

At this point, Vincent realizes he must go back to his beginnings to learn what made him capable of creating such happiness and then destroying it as well. Dark rain begins to fall, mixing with yellow rain in a hallucinatory fantasy until black dominates and a yellow hand wipes the slate clean, giving one last fleeting glimpse of colours, before we fade into a landscape of black and grey.

Sunflowers

August-September, 1887 | Paris, France

Oil on canvas. 61 x 43.2 cm
The Metropolitan Museum of Art
New York, USA

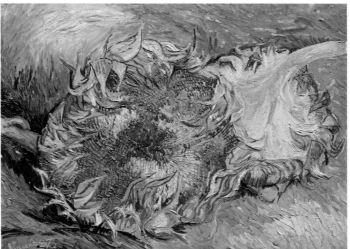

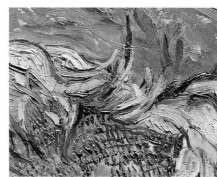

Yellow

An Act of Happiness

The colour breaks forth like an epiphany, appears and disappears inside his mind, like a memory recorded only on canvas.

The sunflowers swarm his memory. They turn into matter, the mind gets overwhelmed by nostalgia.

And while the eyes ask for tears, his fingers move across the colour, tracing paths that move away from the memory.

Vase With Twelve Sunflowers

1888 | Arles, France

Oil on canvas. 72 x 91 cm

Bayerische Staatsgemäldesammluugen
Neue Pinakothek. Munich, Germany

Vase with Fifteen Sunflowers

1888 | Arles, France

Oil on canvas. 73 x 93 cm

National Gallery
London, UK

«Just go and sit outdoors, painting on the spot itself! Then all sorts of things like the following happen.»

Vincent Van Gogh in his letter to Theo Van Gogh, Nuenen, July 14, 1885

The grey vistas and skeletal trees that swim out of the darkness towards us leave little doubt as to what kind of flashback Vincent is experiencing as he looks into his past: a cold, loveless and forbidding period in his life.

The nature of his spiritually stern father and his economically controlling mother find their way into every face he paints. There are no smiles, there is no laughter, there is a deadness behind their eyes. Everyone works, but whether they are at a loom or in the fields, they take no joy in their occupation. It is a duty to be done.

The first light to appear is a candle that allows us to examine the bible, with its relentlessly turning pages.

When it finally fades into the darkness, a shocking image takes its place: a grinning skeleton smoking a cigarette. It's a conspiratorial sort of *momento mori* from an artist who smoked heavily for his whole adult life. Vincent painted it during his unhappy year (1885-1886) studying at the Academy of Fine Arts in Antwerp. During that period, his professors often accused him of not being able to accurately portray human anatomy.

This painting was his sardonic reminder that he knew the human skeleton all too well and the cigarette between its bony lips announces that it is truly a work by Vincent Van Gogh. Then we see a solitary lamp, followed by a plume of smoke from a humble meal of potatoes, being consumed by five working people, a synthesis of all Van Gogh grew up surrounded by. Hundreds of faces, thousands of moments lived in 32 years went into his first great painting. And having created it, that section of his life fades into darkness forever.

Pollard Birches

March, 1884
Nuenen, The Netherlands

Pencil, pen, brush and brown ink on paper. 39.5 x 54.2 cm

Van Gogh Museum
Amsterdam, The Netherlands

Head of a Skeleton with a Burning Cigarette

January-February 1886
Antwerp, Belgium

Oil on canvas. 30.4 x 42.4 cm

Van Gogh Museum
Amsterdam, The Netherlands

Still Life With Bible

April, 1885
Nuenen, The Netherlands

Oil on canvas. 78 x 65 cm
Van Gogh Museum
Amsterdam, The Netherlands

Farmhouse In Nuenen

June-July, 1885 | Nuenen | Oil on canvas. 85 x 60 cm
The Netherlands | Städelsches Kunstinstitut
| Frankfurt am Main, Germany

The Potato Eaters

April, 1885 | Nuenen | Oil on canvas. 114.5 x 81.5 cm
The Netherlands | Van Gogh Museum
| Amsterdam, The Netherlands

Flashback

Nocturne

It's still a memory, made up of thousands of gazes from all the people met.

Every thought brings back a past moment recorded on canvas: hard days, religion mixed with rebellion, a constant feeling of strain in wanting to be accepted as an artist.

A light is alternately cast on his past, just like through a Kantian candle, we are given a chance to see his past, to perceive its shallowness, and get lost in the warm smoke invading the space and holding us like characters of his most important work.

The Potato Eaters will make him aware of being a painter.

«Seemingly there's nothing simpler than painting peasants or rag-pickers and other labourers but —
no subjects in painting are as difficult as those everyday figures!»

Vincent Van Gogh in his letter to Theo Van Gogh, Nuenen, early July, 1885

This is another segment of Vincent's final journey that is metaphorical, rather than literal. Just like the sunflowers of Yellow weren't painted at the beginning of his career, the three paintings used for the visual collages in Dawn and New Life weren't created immediately after his departure from Antwerp, but when he arrived in Arles three years later.

What they do represent, however, is Van Gogh leaving behind the repression and colourless sterility of his early life for a world full of possibilities. Colours in their most extreme form dazzle our eyes. Bold strokes of the paint brush make us almost feel we can touch the wheat fields, embrace the clouds, and be blinded by the sun. And the labourers we see here are not the stooped, servile menials from the past, but proud individuals who stand tall and proud in the work they are doing.

Throughout, Edith Piaf sings "Non, je ne regrette rien," as Vincent embarks on a new life, one he feels he can live with no regrets, no fears. But even here, his hidden passions, his dark repressed emotions begin to break through and the once radiant landscape turns into a lurid red of the imagination as the sun sets, converting everything briefly into a forbidding nightmare world, before fading quickly to black.

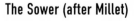

The Sower (after Millet)

Late October, 1889 | Saint Rémy, France

Oil on canvas. 66 x 80.8 cm
Collection Stavros Niarchros
Athens, Greece

The Sower | Oil on canvas. 80.5 x 64 cm

June, 1888 | Arles, France | Kröller-Müller Museum
Otterlo, The Netherlands

Wheat Field with Sheaves | Oil on canvas. 66.6 x 55.2 cm

June, 1888 | Arles, France | Honolulu Academy of Arts
Honolulu, USA

Willows At Sunset | Oil on canvas. 34 x 32 cm

1888 | Arles, France | Kröller-Müller Museum
Otterlo, The Netherlands

Harvest In Provence | Oil on canvas. 60 x 50 cm

June, 1888 | Arles, France | The Israel Museum
Jerusalem, Israel

Dawn and New Life

"Non, je ne regrette rien"

The Sower fully represents the dawn of a new life: lying in a field, he stares at the sun that gets persistently imprinted in the retina of his eyes. A whole day lived by memory, fading into a night that, at an embryonic level, reveals to be so full of light.

«Their story is ours, for we who live on bread, are we not ourselves wheat to a considerable extent?!»

Vincent Van Gogh in his letter to Willemien Van Gogh, Saint-Rémy-de-Provence, July 2, 1889

Paris was the place that would change Vincent's life forever. No longer would he paint the low-hanging skies and claustrophobic buildings of his years in the Low Countries. Paris was the place of vistas, of openness, of a new, clear vision.

This is a city where an artist could wander aimlessly, yet still always discover something worth seeing. Not like the world where Vincent had grown up, driven by religion and work. His colours are still somewhat muted and tentative, forming the bridge between the painter he was and the one he would become. The blues of the sky and the yellows of the buildings are unlike anything he had ever painted in his home country, but they are still far removed from the ones he would employ when he moved south to Arles and truly found his style.

During his years in Paris, he met many artists (Bernard, Toulouse-Lautrec, Signac, Monet) and learned much from watching how they painted and how they lived. "What's to be gained here is progress!" he wrote enthusiastically to a friend back home in Antwerp shortly after his arrival in Paris and he followed the path with intensity.

Although he found a small studio where he continued to work, he soon discovered that this was a city of cafes, where conversation and human contact was as vital as wine and cognac. For the first time, Vincent paints these cafes, tentatively at first, then with increasing confidence, Jovial men and mysterious women begin to inhabit his paintings, as he studies them closely, with an eye that can zoom in for a close-up more telling than any camera. Vincent is learning. Soon he will put those lessons to good use.

Le Moulin de la Galette | Oil on canvas. 46.5 x 38 cm
1886 | Paris, France | Alte Nationalgalerie Berlin, Germany

Quarry At Montmartre | Oil on canvas. 62.5 x 56 cm
Autumn, 1886 | Paris, France | Van Gogh Museum Amsterdam, The Netherlands

The Seine Bridge near Asnieres | Oil on canvas. 73 x 53 cm
1887 | Paris, France | Collection Dominique de Menil Houston, USA

Le restaurant de la Sirène à Asnières | Oil on canvas. 65 x 54 cm
Summer, 1887 | Paris, France | Musée d'Orsay. Paris, France

Paris

It's Better To Go Forward

Paris is not only a destination, but the symbol of a journey of personal growth. A pale light illuminates new colours and new expressive techniques, related to the Impressionist trend.

We pass through the clouds, watch some windmills animated by the wind, we hear the river flowing inside its banks, where passers-by walk without noticing a small man with an easel, painting in the middle of the street. Paris is the place to become great among the great ones.

«There is much to be seen here. I did not even know what the Impressionists were, now I have seen them.»

Vincent Van Gogh in his letter to Horace Mann Livens, Paris, September or October, 1886

If Paris is where Van Gogh began to receive his advanced education in the use of colour, then Japan was his finishing school. But he didn't have to go there, because Japan came to Paris, starting with the 1867 World's Fair. A craze for all things Japanese swept the city. However, unlike similar crazes - this one didn't quickly vanish but took root and flourished.

Although Van Gogh was aware of the craze when he was still in Antwerp and hung copies of Japanese prints on his wall, he arrived in Paris when the period of imitation, known as Japonaiserie, was in full flower. During the fall of 1887, he created several distinct examples of Japonaiserie, most useful for what they taught Van Gogh about the use of colour. For the first time, he used large areas of solid, radiant hues and this enabled him to cross the bridge between what he had learned in Paris and what he would paint in Arles.

The City of Light had taken him away from the murky palate of his youth, but it was in the crucible of Japanese art, with its strict discipline, that we begin to see the use of pure yellow and blue that would dominate so much of the work he painted in the final three years of his life. *Japonaiserie* series works like *Oiran* and *Bridge in the Rain* may seem to be light years away from Van Gogh's more personal works, but look at them closely and you can see the seeds of *The Yellow House*, *Irises* and *The Starry Night*.

The Japanese period provided lessons that Vincent would be able to use as he plunged into the final two and a half years of his life.

Almond Blossom | Oil on canvas. 92 x 74 cm
1890 | Saint Rémy, France | Van Gogh Museum
Amsterdam, The Netherlands

Peach Tree in Blossom |
April-May, 1888 | Arles, France
Oil on canvas. 59.3 x 80.5 cm
Van Gogh Museum
Amsterdam, The Netherlands

Japonaiserie:
Bridge in the Rain | Oil on canvas. 54 x 73 cm
Sept.-Oct., 1887 | Paris, France | Van Gogh Museum
Amsterdam, The Netherlands

Japonaiserie:
Oiran (Courtesan)
September-October, 1887 | Paris, France
Oil on canvas. 60.5 x 105 cm
Van Gogh Museum. Amsterdam
The Netherlands

Japanese Inspiration
"I feel I'm in Japan"

When the Edo period ended in 1868, and Japan opened up to Western culture, Paris got flooded by all sorts of Japanese things. Parisians fell in love with decorative objects and colourful prints engraved on woodblock matrixes called "ukiyo-e", pictures of the floating world.

Van Gogh was captivated by all the elements of this extraordinary visual culture and by the way they could be used for a new way of seeing.

«Japanese art is something like the primitives, like the Greeks, like our old Dutchmen,
Rembrandt, Potter, Hals, Vermeer, Ostade, Ruisdael. It doesn't end.»

Vincent Van Gogh in his letter to Theo Van Gogh, Paris, July 15, 1888

When Vincent arrived in Arles in February, 1888, it almost seemed to him as though it was the place he had wanted to be all of his life. It was small, but not too small, with roughly 50,000 inhabitants. A man could get to know the figures who frequented the bars and restaurants and if Vincent drank too much absinthe on an evening, as he often did, they would help him find his way home.

The countryside around was beautiful and Vincent would discover the depths of its wonders during the summer months. But his first focus was on the town and where he would live. He saw Arles as the center of an artists' colony with himself and Gauguin as its leaders, so their home would have to be perfect.

In May, he rented four rooms in a house that was painted bright yellow, as so many homes in Arles were. Vincent called it "The Yellow House", bestowing special dignity on it and wrote to Theo that "It's tremendous, these yellow houses in the sunlight against the incomparable freshness of the blue sky."

Everything had to be just so: the chairs, the tables, the beds. He painted pictures of almost all of them, as though every detail of this had to be preserved for all posterity. Some might argue the months leading up to Gauguin's arrival were the happiest time in Vincent's life, but wiser eyes could see that he was spinning himself into a manic state that could never have a peaceful ending.

No matter how carefully Vincent decorated the house or how meticulously he furnished it, the walls would soon start closing in on him and Gauguin, with only one possible ending.

The Yellow House

September, 1888 | Arles, France

Oil on canvas. 91.5 x 72 cm
Van Gogh Museum. Amsterdam, The Netherlands

The Bedroom in Arles | Oil on canvas. 90 x 72 cm

October, 1888 | Arles, France | Van Gogh Museum
Amsterdam, The Netherlands

Vincent's Chair | Oil on canvas. 73.5 x 93 cm

December, 1888 | Arles, France | National Gallery
London, UK

The Arrival in Arles

The Yellow House

Not only a room, but the metaphor of a journey undertaken by Vincent because of a big hope: gathering a community of painters under the light of Provence, in order to create and grow together.

We watch him decorating the room. We witness its composition from the very origin, the lines, the perspective, the love he shows in every gesture while creating this very important place.

«I had a new idea in mind, and here's the croquis of it... This time it's simply my bedroom.»

Vincent Van Gogh in his letter to Theo Van Gogh, Arles, October 16, 1888

After moving to Arles early in 1888, he began to paint at a rate that surpassed even his usual intensity, turning out over a hundred canvases in a matter of months. He had always smoked and drank instead of eating and sleeping, but now the pattern spun out of control. Convinced that the arrival of Paul Gauguin in Arles would herald the most important period of his life, he approached everything with a growing manic energy.

When the relationship with Gauguin began to fall apart after a few months, Vincent became even more erratic. On December 23, the two artists quarreled, with Gauguin leaving to spend the night in a hotel. Vincent slashed his left ear off with a razor, wrapped it in a handkerchief and then presented it to a woman who worked at a nearby brothel. The police found him the next morning in a blood-soaked bed. For several weeks, he remained in a state of delirium in the hospital.

He had painted the beauteous scenery of Arles but now, in his maddened state, everything seemed threatening, changing shape in an alarming way, with skies the colour of blood and trees whose branches seemed to be demons intent on strangling him. The sunflowers that were once a symbol of the regard he and Gauguin had for each other were now a confused morass of decaying blossoms.

Only darkness and oblivion would relieve the pain.

Olive Grove | Oil on canvas. 92 x 72 cm

Mid June, 1889 Saint Rémy, France | Kröller-Müller Museum Otterloo, The Netherlands

The Olive Trees | Oil on canvas. 91.4 x 72.6 cm

June-July 1889 Saint Rémy, France | Museum of Modern Art (MoMA) New York, USA

The Olive Tree Pickers | Oil on canvas. 89.9 x 72.4 cm

1889 | Saint Rémy, France | The Metropolitan Museum of Art New York, USA

Red Vineyards at Arles | Oil on canvas. 93 x 75 cm

November 1888 | Arles, France | Pushkin Museum of Fine Arts Moscow, Russia

Nature
Surprise and Inspiration

It is a journey through seasons, from spring to fall, a constant search for the right light, the right strength that nature will impress on his canvas.

In his wandering, the painter discovers a world made of sharp shadows, intense colours, identical yet different shapes that stand out through mighty cypresses and olive tree groves, against a clear sky, constantly transforming the landscape.

«Sometimes I long so much to do landscape, just as one would for a long walk to refresh oneself, and in all of nature, in trees for instance, I see expression and a soul, as it were.»

Vincent Van Gogh in his letter to Theo Van Gogh, The Hague, December 10, 1882

For a while after his release from the hospital Vincent became largely a creature of the night. Haunted by insomnia and paranoid fantasies that people were trying to poison him, he spent more and more time in all-night cafes where he could find some companionship, even of the lowest kind.

His painting now begins to show skies of a blue so dark it is nearly black, with stars trying to break through the bleak surround. We see tables on a cobblestoned terrace, clustered together in the available light, and beyond them, an emptiness that dissolves into a blood-spattered pavement, before becoming the crimson walls of another café.

This is where the dregs of society cling to the walls, hoping no one will notice them, sad faces with empty eyes, gradually being swallowed up by the darkness until only one solitary lamp remains.

And then, once again, darkness.

Portrait of Dr. Gachet

June, 1890
Auvers-sur-Oise, France

Oil on canvas. 57 x 68 cm
Musée d'Orsay
Paris, France

The Café Terrasse on The Place du Forum

September, 1888 | Arles, France

Oil on canvas. 65.5 x 81 cm
Kröller-Müller Museum
Otterloo, The Netherlands

The Night Café in the Place Lamartine in Arles

September, 1888 | Arles, France

Oil on canvas. 89 x 70 cm
Yale University Art Gallery.
New Haven, USA

Madame Ginoux with Gloves and Umbrella

November 1888 | Arles, France

Oil on canvas. 74 x 93 cm
Musée d'Orsay, Paris, France

Back to Arles

Back to Arles – Inside the Cafe

A room full of colours, the light pervading the walls and wrapping us up together with some looming objects...

The lines shatter, perspectives distort themselves: it's the absinthe that is playing games with our minds, lighting up the dark night sky, pervading us with imaginative power. Then the light slowly grows dim, rationality re-emerges and lets a liberating darkness break forth.

«It often seems to me that the night is much more alive and richly coloured than the day.»

Vincent Van Gogh in his letter to Theo Van Gogh, Arles, September 8, 1888

Vincent came to realize that he could not remain in Arles with its intense passions and troubling memories. In a desperate attempt to take some control of his life, he committed himself to the asylum of Saint-Paul de Mausole on May 8, 1889.

In those initial months there, he created some of his most beautiful works, like the studies of irises as well as some of his most magnificent but troubling ones, such as *The Starry Night*. But this was the problem. The times of relative calm and peace between interludes of torment and madness grew shorter and shorter. In this sequence, we see how Vincent's mind was working, with the elements of nature he most loved – the trees and flowers, turning into things that terrified him.

The duality between life and death, sanity and madness, yellow and blue was being played out in a manner that Vincent could no longer understand or control. In February of 1890 he entered into a severe depression which left him for several months barely able to draw or paint.

He convinced himself he needed to leave the asylum and seek alternative care, so in May of 1890, he embarked on the final geographic cure of his life – through fields that still remained blazingly yellow, while the blue skies above them rapidly grew darker and more ominous every day.

Irises

1890 | Saint Rémy, France

Oil on canvas. 92.1 x 73.7 cm
The Metropolitan Museum of Art
New York, USA

Irises

1890 | Saint Rémy, France

Oil on canvas. 73.9 x 92.7 cm
Van Gogh Museum
Amsterdam The Netherlands

Irises

May, 1889 | Saint Rémy, France

Oil on canvas. 93 x 71 cm
J. Paul Getty Museum
Los Angeles, USA

From Earth to Colour

From Earth to Colour – Roots and Irises

An abstract dance, among contorted roots and streams of light, painted in the open air, without hesitation.

There's a lingering sense of death, threatening and growing, yet still, in the last act, we may see the light.

"How well he has understood the exquisite nature of flowers!"

French Art Critic Octave Mirbeau, Paris, 1892

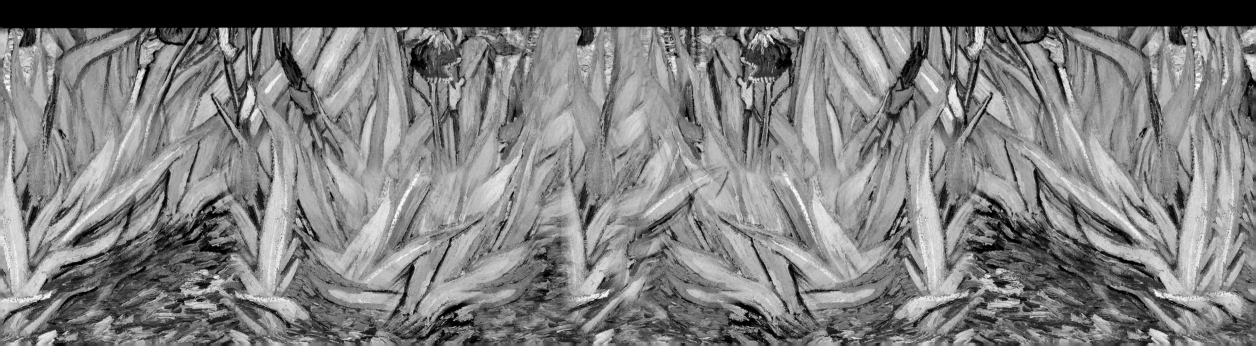

In May of 1890, Vincent arrived in Auvers-sur-Oise, a small community about 25 km northwest of Paris.

At first, the calming effect of a new landscape and the treatment of a new physician, Dr. Paul Gachet, works its magic on Vincent. His paintings seem more tranquil, the colours grow more subdued, and attractive young women replace the night-crawling denizens of his most troubled period. His brother Theo visited Vincent on a tranquil Sunday in June, bringing his wife and infant son. The two brothers remembered it as one of the happiest days they had ever known. And yet, Vincent's mind was still not at rest. His demons were only sleeping and soon they would make their presence felt.

Even ordinary pictures of houses and churches began to be painted in increasingly darker blues. The brush strokes grew bolder and more erratic. The perspective was often ajar. And then he began painting outside of the town, in the wheat fields that had always beckoned him.

"If I am worth anything later," he once wrote, "then I am worth something now. For wheat is wheat, even if people think it is a grass in the beginning." He finished 70 canvases in as many days, lugging his canvases in blazing heat several miles each way. The inspiration never flagged, but the storm clouds never stopped gathering. And then, one day in July, in his monumental *Wheat Field with Crows*, what he had always feared came to the surface.

His normal struggle between yellow wheat and blue skies now had an added ingredient. Crows. Black crows. Scores of them, sweeping across the battleground of his canvas with their twin messages of madness and death.

House and Figure | Oil on canvas. 38.1 x 50.8 cm

1890 | Auvers-sur-Oise, France | The Barnes Foundation
Philadelphia, USA

**Wheatfields
Near Auvers-Sur-Oise** | Oil on canvas. 101 x 50 cm

June, 1890 | Auvers-sur-Oise, France | Österreichische Galerie Belvedere
Vienna, Austria

The Farm In Summer | Oil on canvas. 45 x 38 cm

1890 | Auvers-sur-Oise, France | Van Gogh Museum
Amsterdam, The Netherlands

**The Church
at Auvers-Sur-Oise** | Oil on canvas. 74.5 x 94 cm

1890 | Auvers-sur-Oise, France | Musée d'Orsay
Paris, France

Auvers-sur-Oise

Peaceful And Quiet But...

A small town, remembered through distorted lines transfiguring reality, a map to remember the current distress, but also working as a memory of a time that is already gone. And here comes the omen, like a flock of black crows covering the yellow wheat.

In hectic brush strokes lies the real gesture, all the awareness of the past.

«I too really regretted not being able to come back to Arles to take my leave of you all.»

Vincent Van Gogh in his letter to Joseph Ginoux and Marie Ginoux-Julien, Auvers-sur-Oise, June 11, 1890

In the final weeks of Vincent's life, to the people he encountered daily in Auvers-sur-Oise, his life had a predictable pattern. He would get up every morning, fortify himself with coffee and carry his easel, canvases and paints out to whatever location he had picked for the day.

"Good-bye for today," he wrote in the last letter he ever sent his mother and sister. "I have to go out to work." He would labour in the sun all morning, then return for a midday meal and go back to paint as late into the day as he felt he could. Dinner would follow on his return and then many drinks before he tried to sleep.

But inside his brain, he was still in the asylum in Saint-Rémy-de-Provence that he had left a few months before. Walking in the high-walled courtyard with the other patients, pacing down endless narrow corridors to a room the size of a cell. What he called at times "his sickness", "his malady" or "his disease" had returned... that is, if it had ever really left. And rather than return to that asylum – or another one - he made his choice.

Since his death, experts argue if Vincent was bipolar, schizophrenic, alcoholic, epileptic, or a variety of other diagnoses. The man himself said "The truth is, we can only make our pictures speak." That was from the last letter he wrote – but never sent – to his brother on July 23.

Four days later, Vincent Van Gogh put a revolver to this chest and pulled the trigger.

St. Paul's Hospital

1889 | Saint Rémy, France

Oil on canvas. 48 x 63 cm

Musée d'Orsay
Paris, France

Trees in The Garden of St. Paul's

1889 | Saint Rémy, France

Oil on canvas. 73.3 x 90.2 cm
Hammer Museum
Los Angeles, USA

Corridor/Vestibule in Asylum

October, 1889 | Saint Rémy, France

Oil on canvas. 47 x 61.5 cm
The Museum of Modern Art
New York, USA

Prisoners Exercising (after Gustave Doré)

*10-11 February, 1890
Saint Rémy, France*

Oil on canvas. 64 x 80 cm
Pushkin Museum of Fine Arts,
Moscow, Russia

The Hospitalization
Saint-Rémy-de-Provence

We are locked up behind high walls, in a round and always repeating path; the trapped body wanders relentlessly, the mind is frozen inside the void.

But a thought breaks forth like a kaleidoscope, multiplying the colours, the matter, the spaces. Awareness, in all of its shades, becomes strength.

«So please deliberately forget your sad journey and my illness. Painting is the profession you know,
and my goodness we're perhaps not wrong to try to keep our hearts human.»

Vincent Van Gogh in his letter to Theo Van Gogh, Arles, January 7, 1889

We end with two paintings of Vincent's that combine the colours and themes that obsessed him all of his life and give us some insight into the journey that he took.

The first is *Starry Night Over the Rhone*, which he painted in Arles in September, 1888. It is a symphony of blue, highlighted with splashes of yellow and green, a work so fluid that it is almost impossible to see where the water ends, the land continues and the sky finishes.

The lights on the shore illuminate the river more brightly than the tiny stars up above and – although painted with Van Gogh's distinctive brush strokes – it is far more tranquil than most of his works. Vincent painted this in the early months of his time in Arles, when he still thought everything was possible and his dream of an artists' colony with Gauguin might come true. It is a calm painting, but not necessarily a joyous one.

Compare it with *The Starry Night*, painted in St. Remy only nine months later, in June 1889, shortly after he had entered the asylum there. In this work, the sky dominates and while that brooding, Van Gogh blue still is the major colour, the stars have much more importance. They are giant swirls, illuminating the night sky, painted with the huge, decisive brush strokes that marked so much of his later work.

There is great pain here, and tremendous suffering, but also a spectacular beauty. It takes your breath away, not just for the universe that it depicts, but for what it has cost the artist.

As he wrote in one of his final letters, "I put my heart and soul into my work, and I have lost my mind in the process."

The Starry Night

June 1889 | Saint Rémy, France

Oil on canvas. 92.1 x 73.7 cm
The Museum of Modern Art (MoMA)
New York, USA

Starry Night Over The Rhone

September, 1888 | Arles, France

Oil on canvas. 92 x 72.5 cm
Musée d'Orsay
Paris, France

Meditating on the Landscape
Timeless Beauty

Our work ends with a slow tempo, in a meditative space.

Two different yet similar works of art, both representing the night, the water, the reflection of these perfectly painted stars, almost astronomically precise. We are witnesses to a life lived with passion and unstoppable desire.

We abandon ourselves into this timeless beauty, to real and imagined colours, while two eyes, among consumed candles, bid their farewell, before fading into darkness.

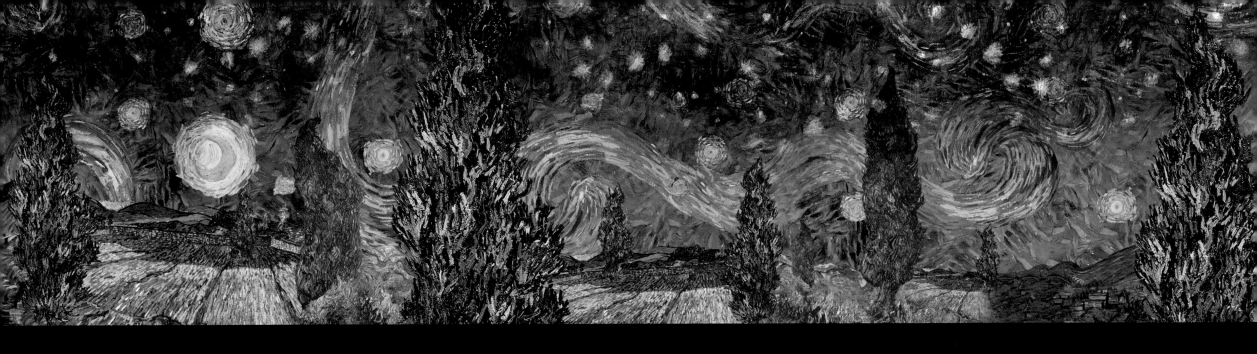

«When I have a terrible need of – shall I say the word – religion, then I go out at night to paint the stars.»

Vincent Van Gogh in his letter to Theo Van Gogh, Arles, September 28, 1888

IMMERSIVE 2020 GOGH BY CAR

Immersive Van Gogh isn't just an extraordinary show opening during extraordinary times, but it led to an extraordinary form of presentation as well.

When Corey Ross and Svetlana Dvoretsky realized that their fantastic new art exhibit was ready to accept visitors before the City of Toronto had come to Stage Two of its Covid-19 reopening process, they wouldn't let it stop them.

"It was more important than ever," said Ross, "to offer a creative outlet for Torontonians to escape and recharge during this unprecedented global crisis."

Back at that initial point in time, in mid-June, visitors were not allowed to walk around the 600,000 cubic foot immersive digital art experience.

But they could drive!

"We believe strongly in the resilience of culture in this great city," affirmed Dvoretsky. And so, they found a solution.

Corey Ross created the first drive-through art exhibition in the world.

Every hour, 10 automobiles were allowed to drive into the space, following strict public safety regulations, then park, turn off their engines and enjoy the glorious vision of Massimiliano Siccardi and Luca Longobardi.

It proved so popular, that viewings were extended until 2:00 AM some evenings and the producers decided to find a way to continue them while still allowing the crowds to visit the exhibit on foot, in socially distanced circles.

Thanks to the superhuman efforts of Slava Zheleznyakov, who managed the construction project, it will now be possible for Torontonians to attend this unique event either with their cars, or without.

Because it doesn't matter how you Gogh, as long as you Gogh.

Corey Ross

Producer

Corey Ross founded Starvox Entertainment in 2005 and has seen it rank on Profit Magazine's list of Canada's top growth companies for five years running – the only live entertainment company ever to place on the list. He has grown the business to a multinational group focused on the production, marketing and distribution of live entertainment, festivals and events.

Mr. Ross produces three shows with Caesars Entertainment in Las Vegas – *The Wow Show* at the Rio and *Extravaganza* and *Potted Potter* at Bally's.

He has also produced *Tropicana de Cuba* in Moscow and the *Mormon Tabernacle Choir* at Carnegie Hall. Other productions have featured such star-power talents as Woody Harrelson, Annie Lennox, Alicia Keyes and Andrea Bocelli.

His theatrical productions include Andrew Lloyd Webber's *Cats* as well as *Forever Plaid*, and *Sherlock Holmes* starring David Arquette. He premiered Trey Parker's *Cannibal: The Musical* and presented the North American premiere of *Bend it Like Beckham: The Musical* in Toronto. Since 2012, Starvox has produced the touring West-End hit show *Potted Potter: The Unauthorized Harry Experience.*

In 2018, Corey created a new division in Starvox Entertainment, devoted to exhibitions – Starvox Exhibits. This division produced the remarkably successful *The Art of Banksy* exhibit in Toronto and Miami and *Immersive Van Gogh* in Toronto.

In 2019, Corey Ross, Svetlana Dvoretsky and Slava Zheleznyakov formed a new company, Lighthouse Immersive, which built a unique art space in Toronto at the historical Toronto Star building, where *Immersive Van Gogh* is being presented.

Immersive Van Gogh

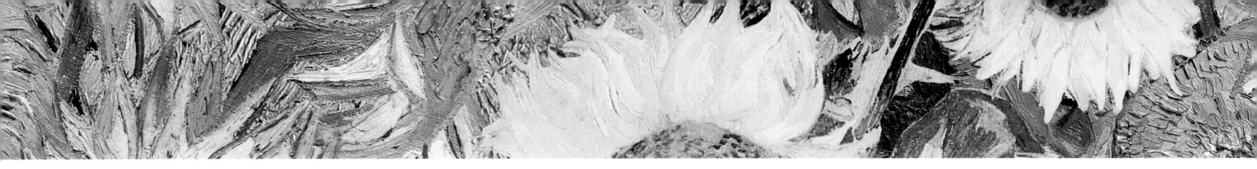

Svetlana Dvoretsky

Producer

Russian born impresario Svetlana Dvoretsky, who formed her company Show One Productions in 2004, has been called "one of the most intuitive impresarios of nowadays" (Toronto Star). Initially focused on classical music and special projects, Svetlana has since expanded her company greatly and has become a leading commercial presenter of international artists, including classical musicians, orchestras, opera stars, theatre, and dance companies.

Svetlana's own training as a classical pianist and her exposure at a young age to a wide range of musicians and other artists inspired her to celebrate them in her chosen calling. Fifteen years later, Show One Productions is collaborating with extraordinary artists from around the world. The company is especially proud of its presentations of *Mikhail Baryshnikov, John Malkovich, Valery Gergiev* and *The Mariinsky Orchestra, Vladimir Spivakov* and *The Moscow Virtuosi,*

The Rotterdam Philharmonic Orchestra and *Yannick Nézet-Séguin, Eifman Ballet,* and *Les Ballets Trockadero de Monte Carlo,* as well as opera stars: sopranos *Sondra Radvanovsky* and *Hibla Gerzmava,* and the late baritone *Dmitri Hvorostovsky. Trio Magnifico* – the historic union at Toronto's Four Seasons Centre for the Performing Arts of soprano *Anna Netrebko* and tenor *Yusif Eyvazov* in their Toronto debuts, with *Hvorostovsky* in his last Toronto appearance – attracted audiences from across the continent and remains an indelible musical memory .

In 2019, together with Corey Ross and Slava Zheleznyakov, Svetlana Dvoretsky formed the company The Lighthouse Immersive, with the clear vision to create a cutting edge art space in which they would present immersive and other types of exhibits and innovative events.

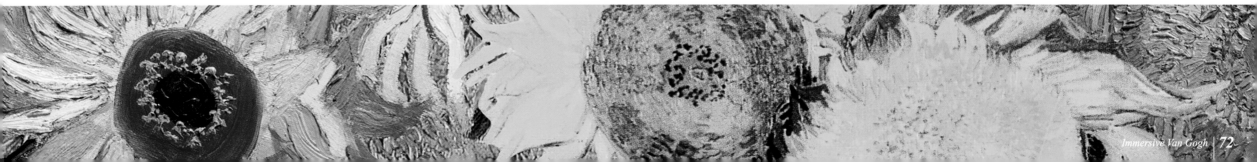

Slava Zheleznyakov

Producer

Slava Zheleznyakov, the Co-Founder of "Lighthouse Immersive", has had a distinguished career of over 25 years. He has specialized in building modern custom developments across Toronto, and recently took on a new challenge of preserving heritage buildings that can be integrated into the city's contemporary landscape. His latest and proudest achievement is the *Immersive Van Gogh Exhibit* – a venture that began by converting a 5-storey industrial base of a 50 year-old high-rise office tower to a magical installation of 600,000 cubic feet projections.

He had to re-develop the existing space into a safe and visually unobtrusive arena for showcasing Van Gogh's work on an astonishing scale. Considering all the supporting elements behind the production, imagination and innovation were at the core. For Slava, the project reached extraordinary heights and expanded beyond anything that has ever been done before. What was once the home to Toronto Star's printing presses was conceptualized into the world's first drive-in art experience.

The old and the new, commerce and culture, architecture and technology – all existing thrillingly, side by side. Slava Zheleznyakov is the man who made it happen.

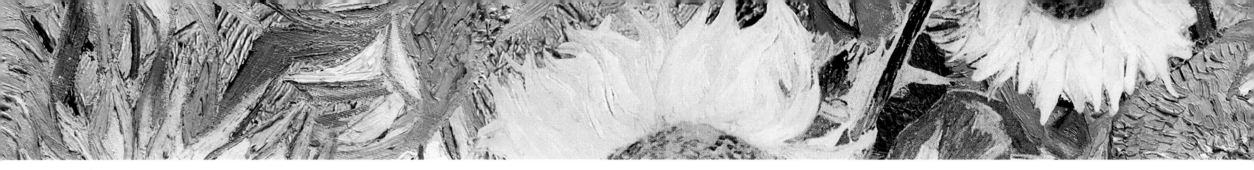

Richard Ouzounian

Writer

"Writing the text for the Immersive Van Gogh Exhibit book has been a pleasure and a privilege. To be so closely involved with the paintings, thoughts and feelings of Vincent at this difficult time in the world's history has enforced my lifelong belief in the power and necessity of art."

– Richard Ouzounian

Richard Ouzounian has worked in the arts professionally for 48 years. During that time, he has directed, written, or performed in nearly 300 shows and had six books published.

He has served as Artistic Director of 5 major Canadian theatres, been an Associate Director of the Stratford Festival of Canada for 4 seasons and was Harold Prince's assistant on the original Toronto production of *The Phantom of the Opera*.

He was Theatre Critic of the Toronto Star, Canada's largest daily newspaper, for 15 years, served as Head of Arts Programming for TVOntario for five years and spent 14 years as the host of CBC Radio's highly popular Broadway program, *Say It With Music*.

Since retiring from The Star in 2015, his stage productions include the Starvox production of *Four Chords and a Gun* in Toronto and Chicago, a 5-person staging of *Candide* for Talk Is Free Theatre and a multi-million dollar production of the Canadian epic, *Napoleon*, in Seoul, South Korea.

In recent years at the Stratford Festival, he has directed *The Fantasticks* starring Eric McCormack, as well as Chilina Kennedy in a newly revised version of Leslie Arden's *The House of Martin Guerre*.

His upcoming projects include an all-star Canadian production of *Follies* in Concert at Koerner Hall for the Royal Conservatory of Music.

Ouzounian lives in Toronto, has been married for 43 years to his wife, Pamela, and has two children, Kat and Michael.

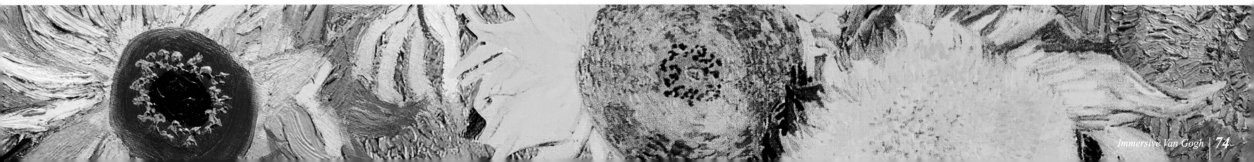

CREDITS

Immersive Van Gogh Exhibit

Directed by
Massimiliano Siccardi

Written by
Massimiliano Siccardi
Vittorio Guidotti
Luca Longobardi

Soundtrack
(musical concept and composition)
Luca Longobardi

VISIONIECCENTRICHE
PRODUCTION

President	**Marco Realino**
Logistic Secretary	**Erica Realino**
Administrative Secretary	**Valeria Garofalo**

L-1S
Graphics and animations

Production Team

Art Director, Producer	**Vittorio Guidotti**
Production manager	**Silvia Caracciolo**
2D animator, producer	**Michele Boncompagni**
2D Animator, Art Director	**Lisa Cantini**
2D / 3D Animator	**Valerio Ciminelli**
2D Animator	**Matteo Inchingolo**
2D Animator	**Daniele Arcuri**
Graphic Designer	**Flavio Lisi**
Graphic Designer	**Francesca Scarponi**

LIGHTHOUSE
IMMERSIVE

Founders and Producers	Corey Ross, Svetlana Dvoretsky, Slava Zheleznyakov
Production / Project Management	Sean Richards
Production	PRG - Branden Charlton, Bobby Klimuszko, Anthony Headley, Chris Arsenault, Jennifer Dymond, George Knuff, Cody Meskey, Simon Clemo, Nick Van Nostrand, Eric Agur
Architecture / Construction	Slava Zheleznyakov, Alex Kachanov - Construction Victor Hipolito - Ambient Design Nick Blais - Lobby design/creative
Marketing	Carla Selzer, Dale Boyer, Vyacheslav Astashevsky, Vassili Goussakov, Patrick Hodgson, Vladimir Kevorkov, Michael Alarewaju
Sponsorship and Government Relationship	Leslie-Ann Dominy
Media Relations	Tran Nguyen, Centric PR
Operations	Jessica Johnston, Natasha Abramova, Valeriy Kostyuk, David Blye, Eugenia Protsko, Anna Mishina, Andrei Mazuruc, Mitch Brown
Ticketing/Box Office Operation	Jonathan Vatinel-Holmes, Farrell Rafferty
Special Thanks to our Supporters and Partners	Pinnacle Corporation and Ralph Montone Production Resource Group
Investors	Alex Shetinin, Cuschieri Family, Badat Family, Kofman Family, Kleiman Family, Sloutsky Family, Nikulin Family
Special Thanks	Derrick Chua, Marc Camilleri, Colm Feore, Vicente Fusco, Len Gill and Marilyn Sherman – Twenty6Two International, Bill Jones, Mary Karelis, Allan Moffatt – Arm and Associates, Corey Nokham - 12thirteen design, Filipe Ferreire, Azra Ross and Shawn Thomson - Epiphany Engineering, Daniela Nardi, Diana Panagiotopoulos, Maia Ross, Steve Radonic, Bob Ramsay, Daniela Sanzone, Kevin Park - KPVM, Snap Hoek Productions, Production Canada

And to all our operational staff

Immersive van GOGH Exhibit

INDEX

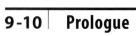

Photo Credits: Vladimir Kevorkov, Patrick Hodgson, Roman Boldyrev

Immersive 2020 - Gogh By Car